Living a
Life of
True Worship

Kay Arthur, Bob & Diane Vereen

PRECEPT MINISTRIES INTERNATIONAL

WATERBROOK
PRESS

LIVING A LIFE OF TRUE WORSHIP
PUBLISHED BY WATERBROOK PRESS
12265 Oracle Boulevard, Suite 200
Colorado Springs, Colorado 80921

All Scripture quotations, unless otherwise indicated, are taken from the New American Standard Bible® (NASB), © Copyright The Lockman Foundation 1960, 1962, 1963, 1968, 1971, 1972, 1973, 1975, 1977, 1995. Used by permission. (www.Lockman.org)

Italics in Scripture quotations reflect the author's added emphasis.

ISBN 978-0-307-45766-0

Published in the United States by WaterBrook Multnomah, an imprint of the Crown Publishing Group, a division of Random House Inc., New York.

WATERBROOK and its deer colophon are registered trademarks of Random House Inc.

Printed in the United States of America
2009

10 9 8 7 6 5 4 3 2 1

SPECIAL SALES
Most WaterBrook Multnomah books are available at special quantity discounts when purchased in bulk by corporations, organizations, and special-interest groups. Custom imprinting or excerpting can also be done to fit special needs. For information, please e-mail SpecialMarkets@WaterBrookMultnomah.com or call 1-800-603-7051.

This small-group study is for people who are interested in learning more about what the Bible says, but who have only limited time to meet together. It's ideal, for example, for a lunch group at work, an early morning men's group, a young mother's group meeting in a home, or a smaller Sunday-school class. (It's also ideal for small groups that typically have longer meeting times—such as evening groups or Saturday morning groups—but want to devote only a portion of their time together to actual study, while reserving the rest for prayer, fellowship, or other activities.)

This book is designed so that all the group's participants will complete each lesson's study activities *at the same time, while you're together.*

However, you'll need a facilitator to lead the group—someone to keep the discussion moving. (This person's function is *not* that of a lecturer or teacher. However, when this book is used in a Sunday-school class or similar setting, the teacher should feel free to lead more directly and to bring in other insights in addition to those provided in each week's lesson.)

If *you* are your group's facilitator, the leader, here are some helpful points for making your job easier:

- Go through the lesson and mark the text before you lead the group. This will give you increased familiarity with the material and will enable you to facilitate the group with greater ease. It may be easier for you to lead the group through the instructions for marking if you as a leader choose a specific color for each symbol you mark.

- As you lead the group, start at the beginning of the text and simply read it aloud in the order it appears in the lesson, including the "insight boxes," which may appear either before or after the instructions or in the midst of your observations or discussion. Work through the lesson together, observing and discussing what you learn. As you read the Scripture verses, have the group say aloud the word they are marking in the text.

- The discussion questions are there simply to help you cover the material. As the class moves into the discussion, many times you will find that they will cover the questions on their own. Remember the discussion questions are there to guide the group through the topic, not to squelch discussion.

- Remember how important it is for people to verbalize their answers and discoveries. This greatly strengthens their personal understanding of each week's lesson. Try to ensure that everyone has plenty of opportunity to contribute to each week's discussions.

- Keep the discussion moving. This may mean spending more time on some parts of the study than on others. If necessary, you should feel free to spread out a lesson over more than one session. However, remember that you don't want to slow the pace too much. It's much better to leave everyone "wanting more" than to have people dropping out because of declining interest.

- If the validity or accuracy of some of the answers seems questionable, you can gently and cheerfully remind the group to stay focused on the truth of the Scriptures. Your object is to learn what the Bible says, not to engage in human philosophy. Really *read* the Scriptures, asking God to show everyone His answers.

LIVING A LIFE OF TRUE WORSHIP

There's a hunger, a quest for the spiritual. Man was made for worship. But worship of whom—or what? Or does it matter as long as a person finds what works for him? Is there a way to worship that is right—and another that is false? Is there a way that will help us develop a genuine, intimate relationship with God?

These are the questions we want to answer as we search out what the Bible has to say about the subject of worship. We are going to take an inductive approach, which means that you will observe the Word of God for yourself. Then, discovering what it says and means, you can determine if you want to order your life according to its truth.

WEEK ONE

OBSERVE

The first place the word *worship* is mentioned in the English Bible is in Genesis 22. Although the word appears only once in that chapter, you can learn some foundational truths about true worship by studying this passage.

Leader: Read aloud Genesis 22:1-10, which you see printed in the sidebar. Have the group say "God" aloud every time He is mentioned. Also have the group...

- *draw a triangle around each occurrence of the word* △**God**△ *(plus all pronouns that refer to Him).*
- *mark the word* **worship** *with a big* **W**.

INSIGHT

Worship is the Hebrew word *shachah* ("a" as in "father" and "ch" as in "Christ"). It means to prostrate oneself or to bow down. In the Old Testament, it is the common term used for coming before God in worship to honor Him. The English word means to look at someone's "worth-ship." To worship God is to respect and honor Him for who He is.

GENESIS 22:1-10

1 Now it came about after these things, that God tested Abraham, and said to him, "Abraham!" And he said, "Here I am."

2 He said, "Take now your son, your only son, whom you love, Isaac, and go to the land of Moriah, and offer him there as a burnt offering on one of the mountains of which I will tell you."

³ So Abraham rose early in the morning and saddled his donkey, and took two of his young men with him and Isaac his son; and he split wood for the burnt offering, and arose and went to the place of which God had told him.

⁴ On the third day Abraham raised his eyes and saw the place from a distance.

⁵ Abraham said to his young men, "Stay here with the donkey, and I and the lad will go over there; and we will worship and return to you."

OBSERVE

When Abraham was seventy-five years old and childless, God told him that He would make of him a great nation through whom all the nations of the earth would be blessed. Isaac, the son God had promised, was born when Abraham was one hundred years old. It was through Isaac that God would give Abraham a land, a nation, and a seed, which according to Galatians 3:16 would be Jesus Christ.

DISCUSS

• What do you learn from marking the references to God?

• What did God instruct Abraham to do?

OBSERVE

*Leader: Read Genesis 22:1-10 again. This time have the group say **Abraham's name** aloud and underline it every time you read his name or a pronoun that refers to him.*

DISCUSS

Look at the references to Abraham that you marked and discuss what you observe about this man from the text.

• What does Abraham do?

• How does he respond to God's command?

• What's his relationship with God? with his son?

• Does anything surprise you about what you read?

OBSERVE

Leader: *Read aloud Genesis 22:1-10 once again. Have the group read aloud with you and mark the phrase* **burnt offering** *like this:* /WV

DISCUSS

• What do you learn from these verses about the burnt offering and how it relates to the act of worship?

6 Abraham took the wood of the burnt offering and laid it on Isaac his son, and he took in his hand the fire and the knife. So the two of them walked on together.

7 Isaac spoke to Abraham his father and said, "My father!" And he said, "Here I am, my son." And he said, "Behold, the fire and the wood, but where is the lamb for the burnt offering?"

8 Abraham said, "God will provide for Himself the lamb for the burnt offering, my son." So the two of them walked on together.

9 Then they came to the place of which God had told him; and Abraham built the altar there and arranged the wood, and bound his son Isaac and laid him on the altar, on top of the wood.

10 Abraham stretched out his hand and took the knife to slay his son.

INSIGHT

The *burnt offering* is described in Leviticus 1. A burnt offering was a voluntary offering, an offering by fire that was a soothing aroma to the Lord. The entire sacrifice (except for the skin) was to be placed on the altar. Nothing was to be held back. When the person offering the sacrifice laid his hand on the head of the sacrifice, it was accepted to make atonement on his behalf.

GENESIS 22:11-19

11 But the angel of the LORD called to him from heaven and said, "Abraham, Abraham!" And he said, "Here I am."

12 He said, "Do not stretch out your hand against the lad, and do nothing to him; for

OBSERVE

Leader: Read 22:11-19 aloud and once again mark...

- *every reference to **God**, including any pronouns or synonyms.*
- *every reference to **the angel of the Lord** with a box, like this:* ☐ *Do not bother to mark synonyms or pronouns for the angel of the Lord.*

DISCUSS

• What did the Angel of the Lord stop Abraham from doing in verses 11 and 12?

• Why did the Angel of the Lord stop Abraham?

• How does this relate to Genesis 22:1 and to what God was doing to Abraham?

• Read the Insight Box on fear and discuss how Abraham showed his fear of God.

INSIGHT

In verse 12, the word *fear* is the Hebrew word *yare* (yaw-ray). In this context it means to have reverence toward God, to trust Him, to respect Him. It does not mean to be afraid of Him. God is reverenced when a person respects Him for who He is. A believer's fear of God is seen when he or she walks in His ways and loves and serves Him in absolute obedience.

---

now I know that you fear God, since you have not withheld your son, your only son, from Me."

13 Then Abraham raised his eyes and looked, and behold, behind him a ram caught in the thicket by his horns; and Abraham went and took the ram and offered him up for a burnt offering in the place of his son.

14 Abraham called the name of that place The LORD Will Provide, as it is said to this day, "In the mount of the LORD it will be provided."

15 Then the angel of the LORD called to Abraham a second time from heaven,

16 and said, "By Myself I have sworn, declares the LORD, because you have done this thing and have not withheld your son, your only son,

17 indeed I will greatly bless you, and I will greatly multiply your seed as the stars of the heavens and as the sand which is on the seashore; and your seed shall possess the gate of their enemies.

18 "In your seed all the nations of the earth shall be blessed, because you have obeyed My voice."

• In verses 15-18, what did the Angel of the Lord tell Abraham that God would do as a result of his obedience? (This is the first time *obey* is used in the Word of God).

Leader: Have the group put a number (1,2,3) with a circle around it to mark each of God's promises to Abraham. See example in verse 17.

OBSERVE

Leader: Read Genesis 22:11-19 again. Once again, have the group mark...

- *every reference to **Abraham**. Remember to also mark any pronouns.*
- *any reference to the **burnt offering** as you did before.*

DISCUSS

• What did Abraham offer to God as a burnt offering?

• According to what you read in verse 14, where did this offering come from?

• What does Abraham learn about God from verse 14?

19 So Abraham returned to his young men, and they arose and went together to Beersheba; and Abraham lived at Beersheba.

• Suppose this incident is a picture of God's love for us. Genesis 22:2 is the first time *love* is used in the Bible, and it's used in connection with a father offering his only son as a burnt offering. We were supposed to die for our sins, but Jesus died in our place. Who provides the ram that dies in Isaac's place? What does this picture for you?

• How does fearing God relate to worship?

WRAP IT UP

If you are going to be a true worshiper of God according to the example of Abraham, what would you need to do? What do you learn about worship from this chapter?

• Using Abraham's life as a pattern, how should you respond to God?

• How does the way you live (or "walk," as the Scripture says) relate to your worship?

• What effect would this have on the way you worship?

If you desire to understand how a sinful person can come into the presence of the Holy God that he or she might have intimacy with Him as never before, then you are going to be so blessed in the weeks ahead as you discover the awesome pattern of worship given to Moses by God.

When you stop and think about the Judeo-Christian faith, it seems incomprehensible that God, the sovereign ruler of all the universe, would desire to have an intimate relationship with those He created. No other faith in the world has such a concept of a God who is so near to those who call upon Him and so desirous of intimacy with His creation, dwelling in their presence.

How does someone worship a God like this? Or does it matter? Can we come to the God of Abraham, Isaac, and Jacob in any way we please? And for those who believe in the Lord Jesus Christ, the Son of the Most High God, what difference does such faith make in approaching our Holy God?

Last week you saw that God gave specific instructions to Abraham regarding how he was to worship Him. Abraham worshiped God by fearing Him, obeying Him, and not withholding from Him someone who was more precious to Abraham than life itself—the son through whom God would make of Abraham a great nation.

This week you'll see that God also gave Moses specific instructions on how His people were to approach Him in worship, even giving him a detailed design for the tabernacle he was instructed to build.

What does the tabernacle have to do with worship? The tabernacle and its layout and furnishings provide a picture of how sinful people come before their Holy God in worship and service. It also provides a picture of Jesus and the true heavenly tabernacle. It illustrates a pattern for how the believer can properly worship God and experience His presence.

EXODUS 25:8-9

8 "Let them construct a sanctuary for Me, that I may dwell among them.

9 "According to all that I am going to show you, as the pattern of the tabernacle and the pattern of all its furniture, just so you shall construct it."

OBSERVE

In Exodus 25, God spoke to Moses regarding the construction of the tabernacle.

Leader: Read aloud Exodus 25:8-9. As you come to a key word that the group should mark, have them say that word aloud.

- *Mark **God** with a triangle as before. Also mark all pronouns that refer to Him.*
- *Mark **pattern** with a squiggly line like this:* ⌒⌒⌒⌒
- *Mark **tabernacle** and **sanctuary** with a rectangle.*

OBSERVE

Now let's gain deeper insight into the tabernacle and its construction by comparing Scripture with Scripture. We'll look at Hebrews 8:1-2 and 8:5, where the author of Hebrews refers to the tabernacle when he speaks of "offering gifts according to the Law."

INSIGHT

The word translated as *tabernacle* in this passage is a noun derived from the Hebrew verb "to dwell." It was the place where God met with man and communicated with him. It was there that man could approach God through a sacrifice.

Leader: Read aloud Hebrews 8:1-2,5 and have the group mark...

- *tabernacle* and *sanctuary*
- *pattern* and *copy*

DISCUSS

- What did God instruct Moses to do? Why?

- What did you learn from marking the tabernacle and pattern in Exodus 25 and Hebrews 8?

HEBREWS 8:1-2,5

1 Now the main point in what has been said is this: we have such a high priest, who has taken His seat at the right hand of the throne of the Majesty in the heavens,

2 a minister in the sanctuary and in the true tabernacle, which the Lord pitched, not man.

5 ...a copy and shadow of the heavenly things, just as Moses was warned by God when he was about to erect the tabernacle; for, "See," He says, "that you make all things according to the pattern which was shown you on the mountain."

EXODUS 40:17-33

17 Now in the first month of the second year, on the first day of the month, the tabernacle was erected.

18 Moses erected the tabernacle and laid its sockets, and set up its boards, and inserted its bars and erected its pillars.

19 He spread the tent over the tabernacle and put the covering of the tent on top of it, just as the LORD had commanded Moses.

20 Then he took the testimony and put it into the ark, and attached the poles to the ark, and put the mercy seat on top of the ark.

OBSERVE

In the section you are about to observe, you will learn about the furniture that God instructed Moses to place in the tabernacle.

Leader: Read Exodus 40:17-33. Mark the following and then look at the drawing opposite the text for a visual picture of what you have read.

- *Underline the phrase **just as the Lord had commanded Moses.***
- *Draw a rectangle around every mention of **tabernacle.***

As you read through the text segment by segment, pause to have the student see where each piece of furniture was placed in the tabernacle. You will see that it begins with the Holy of Holies and moves out from there.

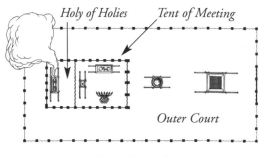

The Tabernacle

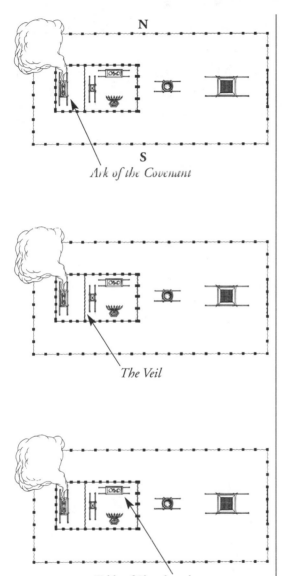

N

S

Ark of the Covenant

The Veil

Table of Showbread

21 He brought the ark into the tabernacle, and set up a veil for the screen, and screened off the ark of the testimony, just as the LORD had commanded Moses.

22 Then he put the table in the tent of meeting on the north side of the tabernacle, outside the veil.

23 He set the arrangement of bread in order on it before the LORD, just as the LORD had commanded Moses.

24 Then he placed the lampstand in the tent of meeting, opposite the table, on the south side of the tabernacle.

25 He lighted the lamps before the LORD, just as the LORD had commanded Moses.

26 Then he placed the gold altar in the tent of meeting in front of the veil;

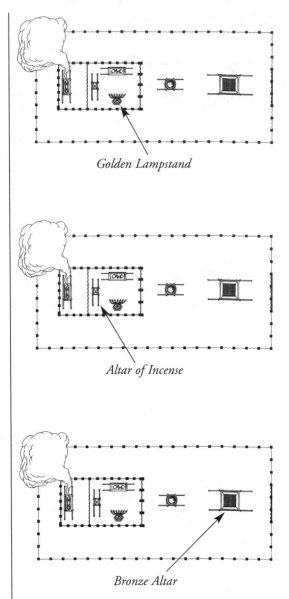

Golden Lampstand

Altar of Incense

Bronze Altar

27 and he burned fragrant incense on it, just as the LORD had commanded Moses.

28 Then he set up the veil for the doorway of the tabernacle.

29 He set the altar of burnt offering before the doorway of the tabernacle of the tent of meeting, and offered on it the burnt offering and the meal offering, just as the LORD had commanded Moses.

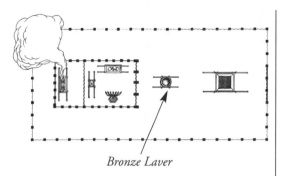

Bronze Laver

DISCUSS

• Quickly review where each piece of the furniture was placed. Do this from the perspective of entering the tabernacle from "the gateway of the court."

• How was the tabernacle to be constructed? Did the people have the freedom to build it any way they desired?

• At this point in our study, does this give you a perspective on the way God is to be worshiped? Do you think God cares how we worship Him?

30 He placed the laver between the tent of meeting and the altar and put water in it for washing.

31 From it Moses and Aaron and his sons washed their hands and their feet.

32 When they entered the tent of meeting, and when they approached the altar, they washed, just as the LORD had commanded Moses.

33 He erected the court all around the tabernacle and the altar, and hung up the veil for the gateway of the court. Thus Moses finished the work.

Exodus 40:34-38

34 Then the cloud covered the tent of meeting, and the glory of the LORD filled the tabernacle.

35 Moses was not able to enter the tent of meeting because the cloud had settled on it, and the glory of the LORD filled the tabernacle.

36 Throughout all their journeys whenever the cloud was taken up from over the tabernacle, the sons of Israel would set out;

37 but if the cloud was not taken up, then they did not set out until the day when it was taken up.

OBSERVE

Now let's observe what happened when Moses finished the work on the tabernacle.

Leader: Read Exodus 40:34-38. Have your group mark...

- *tabernacle* with a rectangle as before
- *tent of meeting* like this:
- *cloud* like this:

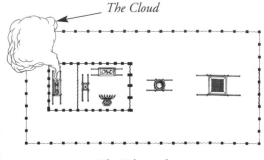

The Cloud

The Tabernacle

DISCUSS

- What happened once all the furniture was placed in the tabernacle and the work was finished?

- What did the cloud represent?

• What do you learn from marking the references to the cloud? Does this relate in any way to what God told Moses He would do in Exodus 25:8—"Let them construct a sanctuary for Me, that I may dwell among them"?

38 For throughout all their journeys, the cloud of the LORD was on the tabernacle by day, and there was fire in it by night, in the sight of all the house of Israel.

OBSERVE

Through this portable tabernacle, God dwelt among His people for almost five hundred years. Then God's presence moved to the temple built—at God's command—by King Solomon.

During the final siege of the Babylonians against Jerusalem in 586 B.C., the cloud of God's presence left Solomon's temple, never to return (Ezekiel 10–11). Solomon's temple was destroyed.

When the Jews returned from the Babylonian exile, the temple was rebuilt. Then, under Roman occupation, Herod refurbished and enlarged the temple. However the cloud of God's presence never again hovered over the Holy of Holies. The glory of His presence was not seen again until…

JOHN 1:1-2,14

1 In the beginning was the Word, and the Word was with God, and the Word was God.

2 He was in the beginning with God....

14 And the Word became flesh, and dwelt among us, and we saw His glory, glory as of the only begotten from the Father, full of grace and truth.

*Leader: Have the group read John 1:1-2,14 aloud, noting the words **dwelt** and **glory**.*

DISCUSS

• According to these verses, where did God's glory now dwell?

• What then would happen when Jesus went into the temple that Herod had refurbished and enlarged (it was referred to as the "Second Temple")?

OBSERVE

Just before Jesus was to be crucified, He gathered His disciples in an upper room and told them that He was going away—back to the Father to prepare a place for them. However, He would not leave them alone. After He ascended to the Father, He would send them the Holy Spirit who would be in them. He said in John 14:23, "If anyone loves Me, he will keep My word; and My Father will love him, and We will come to him and make Our abode with him."

In other words, God would dwell in them—in those who would believe in Him.

Leader: *Read aloud 1 Corinthians 3:16 and 6:19-20. Have the students say the key words they are marking as you read the text. Keep in mind that these verses were written to those who would believe that Jesus Christ is the Son of God.*

    Mark the following:
- ***temple*** *as you marked "tabernacle"*
- ***Spirit of God****—underline it*
- ***dwells in you*** *or* ***in you*** *with a "cloud"*
- ***glorify****—circle it*

DISCUSS

- Where did the glory of God first dwell? Then when was it seen? And finally, where does His Glory, His Spirit now dwell?

- How would understanding all this affect the way you worship God?

1 CORINTHIANS 3:16

Do you not know that you are a temple of God and that the Spirit of God dwells in you?

1 CORINTHIANS 6:19-20

19 Or do you not know that your body is a temple of the Holy Spirit who is in you, whom you have from God, and that you are not your own?

20 For you have been bought with a price: therefore glorify God in your body.

WRAP IT UP

Throughout the Old Testament the glory of the Lord is linked with the presence of God among Israel in the tabernacle. In the New Testament, under the New Covenant, God's glory is revealed by His presence with us.

The tabernacle was a specific dwelling place for God, a place for the cloud of the glory of the Lord by day and for the cloud of fire by night. When the cloud was taken up, the sons of Israel would set out. If the cloud was not taken up, they did not set out. When God moved, the people moved. If He didn't move, they didn't move. For the people, this required unconditional surrender.

• What does it mean that God calls you His temple, and what effect should that have on your life?

• How does this relate to our worship of God? Could it be that worship is more than a time of singing at the beginning of a church service—a worship service?

Next week you will begin to follow the pathway of the priest through the tabernacle, and you will see the role played by each piece of furniture in the tabernacle in bringing man back into a right relationship with God through the forgiveness of sins. If you desire to know the pathway into His presence, be with your group next week.

When Moses went up on Mount Sinai to receive the Ten Commandments, the people could not come with him lest they die. Unholy man could not come into the presence of the Holy God.

Moses spent forty days and nights on the mountain. During that time, God gave him not only the Ten Commandments and the detailed plans for the tabernacle, but also the procedures by which Moses was to anoint, ordain, and consecrate the priests who would minister in the tabernacle.

Man needed a representative. He needed someone who could mediate for him in this new place of worship, someone who could deal with the sacrifices in such a way that God would be satisfied, the offering would be accepted, and man would be restored in his relationship with God. God could then dwell in his midst, and they could commune with each other.

God gave the priest specific instructions as to how and when he would worship God in the tabernacle. The priest didn't have the liberty to devise or implement his own way. Once again, it must be done God's way.

As we observe the priest and his path through the tabernacle, we will see the path we must follow to experience true worship. For the next three weeks we will look at how the priests related to every part of the tabernacle, how this foreshadowed Jesus, and how all this relates to us today.

OBSERVE

According to Exodus 28:1, God said that He was calling Aaron and his descendants to the priesthood in order that they might "minister as priest to Me." The priest was to minister *to God.* To do this then would be worship.

LEVITICUS 9:7

Moses then said to Aaron, "Come near to the altar and offer your sin offering and your burnt offering, that you may make atonement for yourself and for the people; then make the offering for the people, that you may make atonement for them, just as the LORD has commanded."

Leader: Read aloud Leviticus 9:7 and have the group repeat the key word "atonement" and any reference to Aaron the priest.

- *Mark references to **Aaron** with a big **P.***
- *Mark **atonement** with a half circle like this:*

INSIGHT

The word translated as *atonement* means to cover. It's often used for the concept of covering over sin with the blood of a sacrifice that makes it possible for sinful man to approach the Holy God. Under the Old Covenant, the Law, this was accomplished by offering a substitute payment for sin with the blood of an animal.

DISCUSS

• What did you learn from marking the word *atonement*?

• How was atonement made?

OBSERVE

All who served in the tabernacle and later in the temple were to come from the tribe of Levi. The priests were to be Levites descended from the family of Aaron. However, in the fullness of time God would designate another to become a high priest.

*Leader: Read aloud Hebrews 4:14; 5:9-10; and 8:1-2. Have the group mark every reference to **priest** or **minister** (including pronouns) as they did before with a big **P**.*

DISCUSS

• Who is our great High Priest?

• What was Aaron, the high priest, to do?

HEBREWS 4:14

Therefore, since we have a great high priest who has passed through the heavens, Jesus the Son of God, let us hold fast our confession.

HEBREWS 5:9-10

9 And having been made perfect, He became to all those who obey Him the source of eternal salvation,

10 being designated by God as a high priest according to the order of Melchizedek.

HEBREWS 8:1-2

1 Now the main point in what has been said is this: we have such a high priest, who has taken His seat at the right hand of the throne of the Majesty in the heavens,

2 a minister in the sanctuary and in the true tabernacle, which the Lord pitched, not man.

REVELATION 1:5-6

5 ...To Him who loves us and released us from our sins by His blood—

6 and He has made us to be a kingdom, priests to His God and Father—to Him be the glory and the dominion forever and ever. Amen.

• Where is He now?

• What tabernacle did He minister in?

OBSERVE

Aaron and his descendants served as priests in the tabernacle and the temple under the Old Covenant, the Law. Under the New Covenant of grace, Jesus became our High Priest, serving in the true tabernacle in heaven. Now let's look at some New Testament scriptures to find out if there are priests today even though there is no temple (except for our bodies being Jesus' temple if we are true believers).

*Leader: Read aloud Revelation 1:5-6 and 1 Peter 2:9. Have the group mark every reference to **priest** and **priesthood** as you marked "priest" earlier.*

DISCUSS

• According to the verses you just observed, who are priests—and to whom?

• Would knowing this affect in any practical way the manner in which you worship God? How?

• What are we to proclaim? Would you consider this worship?

1 PETER 2:9

But you are a chosen race, a royal priesthood, a holy nation, a people for God's own possession, so that you may proclaim the excellencies of Him who has called you out of darkness into His marvelous light.

OBSERVE

Last week you saw there was only one way to enter the tabernacle—through the "gateway of the court," which was always to the east. What is the picture that God wants us to see in this pattern?

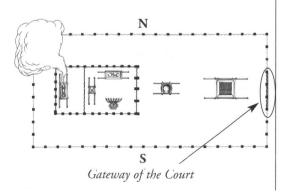

Gateway of the Court

JOHN 10:9

[JESUS IS SPEAKING.]

"I am the door; if anyone enters through Me, he will be saved, and will go in and out and find pasture."

JOHN 14:6

Jesus said to him, "I am the way, and the truth, and the life; no one comes to the Father but through Me."

Leader: Read John 10:9 and 14:6 in order to see how this part of the tabernacle is fulfilled in Jesus.

- *Mark every reference to **Jesus,** including pronouns, with a cross.*

DISCUSS

- What do you learn about Jesus from these verses?

- How does this fit with what you learned about the "gateway of the court"?

- How would this apply to worshiping God? Can a person worship God correctly apart from Jesus Christ?

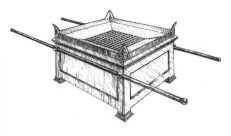

The Bronze Altar

OBSERVE

Leader: *Have the group look at the diagram of the tabernacle to see again the location of the bronze altar.*

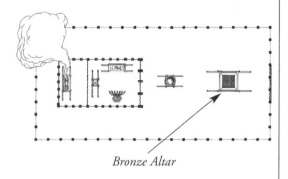

Bronze Altar

The first thing the worshiper encountered after entering the door of the tabernacle was the bronze altar. The first nine chapters of Leviticus cover the seven different offerings that could be offered upon the bronze altar; however, we will look at only one.

Leader: *Read aloud Leviticus 1:2-5.*
- *Circle every reference to the **person** bringing the offering.*
- *Mark **burnt offering** like this:* **MWV**
- *Mark every reference to **priest** with a **P** as before.*
- *Mark **atonement** with a half circle as before.*

LEVITICUS 1:2-5

2 ..."When any man of you brings an offering to the LORD, you shall bring your offering of animals from the herd or the flock.

3 If his offering is a burnt offering from the herd, he shall offer it, a male without defect; he shall offer it at the doorway of the tent of meeting, that he may be accepted before the LORD.

4 He shall lay his hand on the head of the burnt offering, that it may be accepted for him to make atonement on his behalf.

5 He shall slay the young bull before the LORD; and Aaron's sons the priests shall offer up the blood and sprinkle the blood around on the altar that is at the doorway of the tent of meeting."

JOHN 1:29

The next day he [John the Baptist] saw Jesus coming to him and said, "Behold, the Lamb of God who takes away the sin of the world!"

HEBREWS 10:4-12

4 For it is impossible for the blood of bulls and goats to take away sins.

5 Therefore, when He comes into the world, He says,

DISCUSS

• What was the procedure for the person bringing the burnt offering? (To answer this you could have someone demonstrate it quickly—it will be more memorable.)

• Where was this offering to be made?

• What was done with the blood of the offering?

• Since the bronze altar is the first piece of furniture in the tabernacle, does this tell you anything about how one approaches God to worship Him?

OBSERVE

Leader: Read aloud John 1:29 and Hebrews 10:4-12.

• *Mark every reference to **Jesus,** including pronouns, with a cross.*
• *Mark **sacrifices, offerings** and **burnt offerings** in the same way you marked "burnt offering" earlier.*
• *Mark every reference to **sin** with a big **S.***

• *Mark any reference to **time** with a clock like this:* 🕐

DISCUSS

• What do you learn from marking *Jesus?*

• Why did Jesus have to die, to offer His body as a sacrifice?

• What did Jesus' offering of His body accomplish? For how long?

• What in the tabernacle would give us a picture of the cross? How?

• What do you learn from this in respect to worshiping God, especially if everything in the tabernacle leads to the ark of the covenant and the mercy seat in the Holy of Holies?

"Sacrifice and offering
You have not desired,
But a body You have
prepared for Me;

6 In whole burnt
offerings and sacrifices
for sin You have taken
no pleasure.

7 "Then I said,
'Behold, I have come
(In the scroll of the
book it is written of
Me) to do Your will,
O God.'"

8 After saying above,
"Sacrifices and offer-
ings and whole burnt
offerings and sacrifices
for sin You have not
desired, nor have You
taken pleasure in them"
(which are offered
according to the Law),

9 then He said, "Behold, I have come to do Your will." He takes away the first in order to establish the second.

10 By this will we have been sanctified through the offering of the body of Jesus Christ once for all.

11 Every priest stands daily ministering and offering time after time the same sacrifices, which can never take away sins;

12 but He, having offered one sacrifice for sins for all time, sat down at the right hand of God.

Exodus 30:18-20

18 "You shall also make a laver of bronze, with its base of bronze,

The Bronze Laver

OBSERVE

Leader: Have the group look at the diagram of the tabernacle to see again the location of the bronze laver. Then read Exodus 30:18-20.

As you read the text, have the group mark…

- *every reference to **Aaron** or **his sons** in the same way you marked "priest," with a **P**.*
- *the **bronze laver** by underlining it.*
- ***water** like this:* 〰〰〰

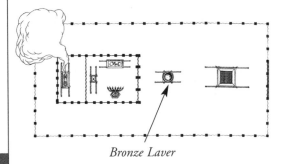

Bronze Laver

DISCUSS

- What was the purpose of the bronze laver?

• Who used it and when?

• Why was it used, and what happened if they didn't wash?

• What does this tell you about worshiping a holy God?

OBSERVE

Now let's look at some passages that will throw greater light on the picture given us in the bronze laver.

Leader: Read aloud Psalm 24:3-4; Ephesians 5:25-26; and 1 John 1:9.
   • *Mark every reference to clean, cleanse, or washing of water.*
   • *Mark every reference to Jesus Christ in Ephesians 5:25-26.*

INSIGHT

The Greek word translated as *sanctify* means "to make holy." When something is holy, it is consecrated, dedicated or set apart for God.

for washing; and you shall put it between the tent of meeting and the altar, and you shall put water in it.

19 "Aaron and his sons shall wash their hands and their feet from it;

20 when they enter the tent of meeting, they shall wash with water, so that they will not die; or when they approach the altar to minister, by offering up in smoke a fire sacrifice to the LORD."

PSALM 24:3-4

3 Who may ascend into the hill of the LORD? And who may stand in His holy place?

4 He who has clean hands and a pure heart, who has not lifted up his soul to falsehood and has not sworn deceitfully.

EPHESIANS 5:25-26

25Husbands, love your wives, just as Christ also loved the church and gave Himself up for her,

26 so that He might sanctify her, having cleansed her by the washing of water with the word.

1 JOHN 1:9

If we confess our sins, He is faithful and righteous to forgive us our sins and to cleanse us from all unrighteousness.

DISCUSS

• Who can approach a holy God? Who can stand in His presence?

• Why did Jesus give Himself up for us— why did He die on a cross?

• We know we have forgiveness of sins through the shedding of Jesus' blood, but is there another form of cleansing that takes place in our lives after we become God's children by faith in Jesus Christ? What does Ephesians 5:25-26 tell us?

• When we sin as a believer, what is our responsibility, according to 1 John 1:9?

• And what will God do?

• From all you have seen, do you think you can worship God apart from being cleansed—clean?

• If you attend a worship service in song and you raise hands to God in praise, what should be the condition of those hands? How would you meet that condition?

WRAP IT UP

Now let's wrap up this week by doing the following exercise as a fitting reminder of the truths we've observed this week in our study of true worship.

Remember that the word *worship* basically means to bow down. It is to look at someone's worth and act or behave accordingly.

The passage you are about to read from Romans 12 follows a full explanation by Paul of the gospel of Jesus Christ—His death and resurrection and its practical implications in our lives. Paul presents this profound explanation in the first eleven chapters of Romans. The twelfth chapter then begins with a term of conclusion: "Therefore."

Leader: *Read Romans 12:1 aloud as a group.*
- *Mark any reference to **sacrifice** as you marked "burnt offering."*
- *Mark the word **worship** with a big* **W.**

As Paul brings the explanation of the gospel to a conclusion, he calls his readers to commitment—commitment in light of the great sacrifice Jesus Christ has made on our behalf at the cross of Calvary.

ROMANS 12:1

Therefore I urge you, brethren, by the mercies of God, to present your bodies a living and holy sacrifice, acceptable to God, which is your spiritual service of worship.

- What is the commitment that we are called to? How does Romans 12:1 describe this sacrifice?

- Is it a command—or a request? And on what basis?

- Do you think true worship can ever happen without our responding to the truth of Romans 12:1?

- What is the most significant insight you have gained regarding worship this week—or these past three weeks?

It would be good to take a few minutes and talk with God about all you've seen this week, if you're comfortable doing this as a group. Worship Him in truth—the truths that you've seen in His Word.

The earthly tabernacle was a shadow of a heavenly tabernacle—a picture of how man can worship God in spirit and in truth. As we continue to evaluate how each piece of furniture in the tabernacle foreshadowed the Savior, we can better understand how to live a life of true worship.

The tabernacle had two major components: the outer court and the tent of meeting (although at times you will find the Scriptures referring to the entire tabernacle as the tent of meeting). The tent of meeting (the inside tent) was further divided into two areas: the holy place and the Holy of Holies. Last week we looked at the items in the outer court: the gateway of the court, the altar, and the laver. This week we'll look at the furnishings in the holy place—the table of showbread, the lampstand, and the altar of incense.

In last week's lesson, we saw how the priest entered the gate, went to the altar (where he made the sacrifices for himself and the people), and washed in the laver. This shows us a pattern of how sinful man approaches God. God provided only one way to come to Him and that is through the door—and Jesus is the door. The door to the tabernacle was always to the east, in the light of the rising sun. Initially, we come to God to be cleansed from our sin through a sacrifice. Therefore the altar becomes the picture of the crucifixion of Jesus Christ. Then we continue the sanctification process of being holy through the cleansing power of His Word and by prompt confession of our sins.

As we continue to follow the way of the priest, we now go with him into the tent of meeting, the holy place. Here immediately to his right the priest would see the table of showbread.

The Table of Showbread

LEVITICUS 24:5-9

5 "Then you shall take fine flour and bake twelve cakes with it; two-tenths of an ephah shall be in each cake.

6 "You shall set them in two rows, six to a row, on the pure gold table before the LORD.

7 "You shall put pure frankincense on each row that it may be a memorial portion for the bread, even an offering by fire to the LORD.

8 "Every sabbath day he shall set it in order before the LORD continually; it is an everlasting covenant for the sons of Israel.

OBSERVE

Look at the tabernacle diagram and locate the holy place and the table of showbread.

Leader: Read aloud Leviticus 24:5-9 and Exodus 25:30.

- *Draw a circle around every reference to the **cakes** or **bread**.*
- *Underline every reference to **holy**.*
- *Mark every reference to **time** with a clock like this:* 🕐

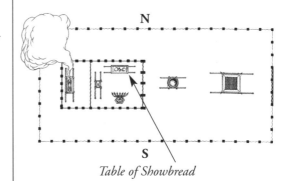

Table of Showbread

INSIGHT

Showbread comes from a Hebrew word that means "bread of the face" or "bread of the presence." In fact, in Exodus 25:30, "Presence" is literally "Face." The showbread was set on the golden table before the face, or presence, of God, who dwelt in the Holy of Holies, just on the other side of the veil.

9 "It shall be for Aaron and his sons, and they shall eat it in a holy place; for it is most holy to him from the LORD's offerings by fire, his portion forever."

EXODUS 25:30

"You shall set the bread of the Presence on the table before Me at all times."

DISCUSS

• What did you learn about the bread? Discuss where it was put, when it was eaten, and where and by whom it was eaten.

• What do you learn from marking the references to time?

OBSERVE

Now we want to see what the bread symbolized—the picture it painted and how it pertains to worshiping God.

JOHN 6:35,48-51

35 Jesus said to them, "I am the bread of life; he who comes to Me will not hunger, and he who believes in Me will never thirst....

48 "I am the bread of life.

49 "Your fathers ate the manna in the wilderness, and they died.

50 "This is the bread which comes down out of heaven, so that one may eat of it and not die.

51 "I am the living bread that came down out of heaven; if anyone eats of this bread, he will live forever; and the bread also which I will give for the life of the world is My flesh."

Leader: Read aloud John 6:35,48-51. Have the group...
- *mark every reference to **Jesus**.*
- *mark every reference to **bread** including pronouns.*
- *put a clock over every reference to **time**.*

DISCUSS

• What did you learn from marking the words *bread* and *Jesus*?

• What are the promises connected with eating this bread?

• You've seen that Jesus is the bread of life. Do you see any parallels or contrasts between Jesus and the manna?

OBSERVE

Leader: Read Matthew 4:1-4 together as a group, along with Deuteronomy 8:3, the text Jesus quotes in Matthew 4.

• Once again mark every reference to **bread.**

INSIGHT

Manna was a type of bread that "rained from heaven" every day except on the Sabbath. It was "like coriander seed, white, and its taste was like wafers with honey" (Exodus 16:31). It was the food that sustained the children of Israel nutritionally during their forty years of wandering in the wilderness. The manna would appear early in the morning, covering the ground like dew. The children of Israel were instructed to gather enough daily for their family. The manna could not be kept overnight except on the sixth day, when they were to gather a two-day supply since no manna came down on the Sabbath.

MATTHEW 4:1-4

1 Then Jesus was led up by the Spirit into the wilderness to be tempted by the devil.

2 And after He had fasted forty days and forty nights, He then became hungry.

3 And the tempter came and said to Him, "If You are the Son of God, command that these stones become bread."

4 But He answered and said, "It is written, 'Man shall not live on bread alone, but on every word that proceeds out of the mouth of God.'"

DEUTERONOMY 8:3

"He humbled you and let you be hungry, and fed you with manna which you did not know, nor did your fathers know, that He might make you understand that man does not live by bread alone, but man lives by everything that proceeds out of the mouth of the LORD."

DISCUSS

Once again you see God giving us pictures in the Old Testament of eternal truths.

• Why won't Jesus yield to the devil's suggestion since Jesus has the power to turn the stones into bread?

• What does Jesus compare the manna to when He addresses the Devil?

• What is the lesson—the application—for us?

• What are the truths pictured in the table of showbread that would help us worship God in the right way? Note who ate "the bread of the Face."

• Do you see any correlation between worship and the Word of God?

• When in church does worship begin and end?

The Golden Lampstand

OBSERVE

Once again look at the drawing of the tabernacle to locate the placement of the lampstand on the south side of the tent of meeting. The golden lampstand was the only source of light in the holy place.

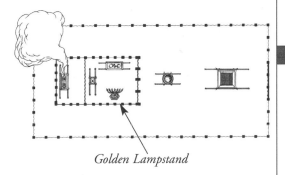

Golden Lampstand

Leader: *Read Leviticus 24:2-3 aloud and have the group call out the key words as they are read.*

- *Mark every occurrence of the word* **lamp** *like this:* ▯
- *Also mark any* **time** *phrases with a clock.*

LEVITICUS 24:2-3

2 "Command the sons of Israel that they bring to you clear oil from beaten olives for the light, to make a lamp burn continually.

3 "Outside the veil of testimony in the tent of meeting, Aaron shall keep it in order

from evening to morning before the LORD continually; it shall be a perpetual statute throughout your generations."

JOHN 1:1-4,9

¹ In the beginning was the Word, and the Word was with God, and the Word was God.

² He was in the beginning with God.

³ All things came into being through Him, and apart from Him nothing came into being that has come into being.

DISCUSS

• What did you learn about the golden lampstand?

• What was to burn in the lamp? Where did it come from?

• How long was it to burn? Who was responsible to see that it kept burning?

OBSERVE

Leader: Read aloud John 1:1-4,9; 8:12; and Ephesians 5:8.

    • *Mark every reference to **Jesus** (including **Word**) with a cross.*

    • *Mark every reference to **light** with a circle.*

DISCUSS

• According to what you have observed and marked in these verses, who is the true Light?

• What does Jesus do for men?

• What do you learn about those who follow Jesus Christ?

• Do you see any significance in these verses and the fact that the only light in the holy place was from the lampstand?

• How does the lampstand in the tabernacle give us a picture of Jesus Christ?

• Do you see any relationship between "walking in the light" and living a life of true worship?

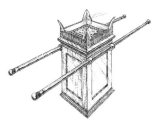

The Altar of Incense

OBSERVE

Look again at the drawing of the tabernacle and locate the altar of incense. (Note that this is a different altar from the one where the sacrifices were made.)

4 In Him was life, and the life was the Light of men....

9 There was the true Light which, coming into the world, enlightens every man.

JOHN 8:12

Then Jesus again spoke to them, saying, "I am the Light of the world; he who follows Me will not walk in the darkness, but will have the Light of life."

EPHESIANS 5:8

...for you were formerly darkness, but now you are Light in the Lord; walk as children of Light.

Exodus 30:1,6-10

1 "Moreover, you shall make an altar as a place for burning incense; you shall make it of acacia wood....

6 "You shall put this altar in front of the veil that is near the ark of the testimony, in front of the mercy seat that is over the ark of the testimony, where I will meet with you.

7 "Aaron shall burn fragrant incense on it; he shall burn it every morning when he trims the lamps.

8 "When Aaron trims the lamps at twilight, he shall burn incense. There shall be perpetual incense before the LORD throughout your generations.

Leader: Read Exodus 30:1,6-10.

- *Mark every reference to the **altar** (including pronouns) with a box, like this:*

- *Mark every occurrence of the word **incense,** like this:*
- *Put a clock over every reference to **time.***

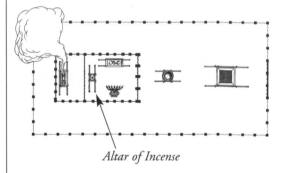

Altar of Incense

DISCUSS

- What do you learn about the altar of incense and its purpose? What was forbidden at this altar?

- What do you learn from marking every reference to incense?

OBSERVE

The high priest would only enter into the Holy of Holies (which we will study next week) through the veil one time a year. This was on the Day of Atonement (Yom Kippur), as explained in Leviticus 16. Remember that until the Babylonian destruction of the temple in 586 B.C., the glory of God filled the Holy of Holies.

The next verses we observe will tell us the role played by the altar of incense on Yom Kippur, the Day of Atonement.

Leader: Read Leviticus 16:12-13.
• *Again have the group mark the words **incense** and **altar.***

DISCUSS

• What did the priest do with the coals, and why?

• What would happen if no incense was taken inside the veil?

• What does this teach you about worshiping the Holy God?

9 "You shall not offer any strange incense on this altar, or burnt offering or meal offering; and you shall not pour out a drink offering on it.

10 "Aaron shall make atonement on its horns once a year; he shall make atonement on it with the blood of the sin offering of atonement once a year throughout your generations. It is most holy to the LORD."

LEVITICUS 16:12-13

12 "He shall take a firepan full of coals of fire from upon the altar before the LORD and two handfuls of finely ground sweet incense, and bring it inside the veil.

13 "He shall put the incense on the fire before the LORD, that the cloud of incense may cover the mercy seat that is on the ark of the testimony, otherwise he will die."

LUKE 1:8-11

8 Now it happened that while he was performing his priestly service before God in the appointed order of his division,

9 according to the custom of the priestly office, he was chosen by lot to enter the temple of the Lord and burn incense.

10 And the whole multitude of the people were in prayer outside at the hour of the incense offering.

Leader: It would be good to have one of the group demonstrate the procedure laid out in these verses.

OBSERVE

There are two New Testament passages we want to look at that will give us insight into the relationship between the altar of incense and prayer.

Leader: Read aloud Luke 1:8-11, an account of what Zacharias was doing when God spoke to him about the birth of his son, John (the Baptist). Also read Revelation 8:3-4.

- *Mark **incense** as you did previously.*
- *Mark **prayer** with an arrow, like this:↑*
- *Mark every reference to **time** with a clock like this: ⏰*

DISCUSS

- What was Zacharias doing, and why?

• What were the people doing at the same time?

• What did you learn about the altar of incense and prayer in Revelation 8:3-4?

• What insights, if any, does this give you in respect to worship?

OBSERVE

Everything in the tabernacle was made after a pattern of things in heaven. Therefore everything is a picture of how we worship the Holy God—and a picture of something else...

Leader: Read aloud Hebrews 7:24-25.
- *Mark every reference to **Jesus** with a cross.*
- *Mark every reference to **time** with a clock like this:* 🕐
- *Mark **therefore**, a term of conclusion, with three dots like this:* ∴

REVELATION 8:3-4

11 And an angel of the Lord appeared to him, standing to the right of the altar of incense.

3 Another angel came and stood at the altar, holding a golden censer; and much incense was given to him, so that he might add it to the prayers of all the saints on the golden altar which was before the throne.

4 And the smoke of the incense, with the prayers of the saints, went up before God out of the angel's hand.

HEBREWS 7:24-25

24 But Jesus, on the other hand, because

He continues forever, holds His priesthood permanently.

25 Therefore He is able also to save forever those who draw near to God through Him, since He always lives to make intercession for them.

PSALM 141:2

May my prayer be counted as incense before You; the lifting up of my hands as the evening offering.

REVELATION 5:8

When He had taken the book, the four living creatures and the twenty-four elders fell down before the Lamb, each one holding a harp and golden

DISCUSS

• What do you learn about Jesus Christ from these verses?

• What do you learn from marking references to time? How does this compare with how long the incense was to burn?

• What does the altar of incense picture for us in the life and work of our Lord Jesus Christ?

OBSERVE

Leader: Read Psalm 141:2; Revelation 5:8; and 1 Thessalonians 5:17.
  • *Mark every reference to **prayer:***
  • *Mark every reference to **incense:***
  • *Put a clock around every reference to time.*

DISCUSS

• What is the connection between incense and prayer in these verses?

- If the four living creatures and the twenty-four elders are falling down before the Lamb, what are they doing?

- The verse from 1 Thessalonians is a command. How do you think this command is to be obeyed—in practical terms—as we go about our day? Do you see any parallel with this command and the burning of incense and the continuing work of Jesus right now at the right hand of the Father?

- What do you learn about prayer and worship from these words?

bowls full of incense, which are the prayers of the saints.

1 THESSALONIANS 5:17

Pray without ceasing.

WRAP IT UP

What did you learn about worship as you studied the table of show-bread, the golden lampstand, and the altar of incense? Which of these spoke to you the most about worshiping God in spirit and truth?

Let's review what we saw:

- *Jesus is the true bread of life.* If you are to worship Him as such, if you are to honor and respect the Father and the Son, are you giving the Word of God the proper place of priority in your life? Do you have time for everything but the Word of God? If so, can you say you are worshiping God in truth? When you go to church to worship God, what place is the Word of God given in the service?

- *Jesus is the true light.* Where are you walking? Are you walking as He walked or are you stumbling in the darkness? Does your walk testify of your fear, your respect, your trust of God? Does it show you to be a true worshiper of God?

- *Jesus is our High Priest.* In the circumstances, difficulties and temptations of life, do you remember that He is interceding for you at that very moment? And do you in turn stay in constant communion with Him committing everything to Him in prayer? Do you worship God by talking everything over with Him, seeking His help and direction? Is He always on your mind?

Are you daily walking the way of the priest? From your study this week, what changes, if any, has God shown you that you need to make in your life?

Leader: Discuss with your group how the table of showbread, the golden lampstand, and the altar of incense relate to a life of true worship. You may want to "pray your way through the tabernacle," worshiping God as you thank Him for being the light, the bread of life, and the one who is always interceding for us.

Last week you saw that the furnishings in the holy place give us a beautiful picture of the work of Jesus Christ and how we are to worship our Holy God.

- Jesus is the bread of life, and we are to feed upon His word.
- Jesus is the light, and we are to walk in His light as children of light in this world so that men can see our good works and glorify our Father in heaven.
- Jesus is our intercessor, always praying for us. There is no trial, testing, or temptation that we cannot bear, for His intercession sustains us and shows us His "way of escape." And because the incense on the altar burned perpetually, so we are never to cease praying, continually offering up a sweet-smelling aroma of the incense of our prayers.

This, beloved of God, is an integral part of worship.

This week we are going to learn about the holiest part of tabernacle, the Holy of Holies. This is where God dwelt, as we have seen, in the cloud of His presence. This would be the place where God and man would meet and commune. God would come down in this specific place and speak to man.

What a God! We could not go to Him so He came down to us.

Exodus 26:31-33

31 "You shall make a veil of blue and purple and scarlet material and fine twisted linen; it shall be made with cherubim, the work of a skillful workman.

32 "You shall hang it on four pillars of acacia overlaid with gold, their hooks also being of gold, on four sockets of silver.

33 "You shall hang up the veil under the clasps, and shall bring in the ark of the testimony there within the veil; and the veil shall serve for you as a partition between the holy place and the holy of holies."

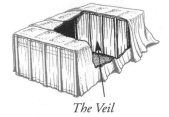

The Veil

OBSERVE

Look at the drawing of the tabernacle to see the placement of the veil. As you do, remember all this was made according to the pattern of the true tabernacle in heaven.

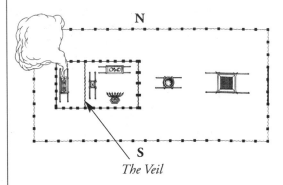

The Veil

Leader: *Read Exodus 26:31-33.*

• *Have the group mark every mention of the **veil** with a **V**.*

DISCUSS

• What do you learn from marking the references to the veil?

• What was the purpose of the veil?

• What furniture was on each side of the veil in the tent of meeting?

OBSERVE

Each piece of furniture in the tabernacle was a picture of Jesus Christ. What then did the veil picture for us?

Leader: Read Hebrews 10:19-20. In this passage you will see that at times the Holy of Holies is referred to as the "holy place."
  • *Mark every reference to **Jesus** with a cross.*
  • *Also mark every reference to the **veil**.*

DISCUSS

• According to Hebrews 10, what does the veil represent?

• When we enter through the veil, where do we enter? How do we enter there?

• What kind of a way is this?

HEBREWS 10:19-20

19 Therefore, brethren, since we have confidence to enter the holy place by the blood of Jesus,

20 by a new and living way which He inaugurated for us through the veil, that is, His flesh....

Exodus 25:10-15,17-22

10 "They shall construct an ark of acacia wood two and a half cubits long, and one and a half cubits wide, and one and a half cubits high.

11 "You shall overlay it with pure gold, inside and out you shall overlay it, and you shall make a gold molding around it.

12 "You shall cast four gold rings for it and fasten them on its four feet, and two rings shall be on one side of it and two rings on the other side of it.

13 "You shall make poles of acacia wood and overlay them with gold.

To understand why it is a new and living way, we need to proceed in our study to the ark of the covenant and then to the Day of Atonement, Yom Kippur.

The Ark of the Covenant and the Mercy Seat

OBSERVE

Look at the drawing of the tabernacle on page 59 and note where the ark of the covenant is situated in the tent of meeting.

On top of the ark was the mercy seat, which had above it the two cherubim of gold, one at each end.

Leader: *Read aloud Exodus 25:10-15,17-22.*

- *Mark every **I** with a triangle since it is God who is speaking in these verses.*
- *Mark every occurrence of **ark** with a rectangle.*
- *Mark every reference to the **mercy seat** with dots to represent blood, like this: mercy seat*

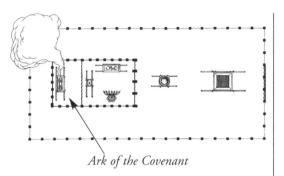

Ark of the Covenant

DISCUSS

• What do you learn from marking the references to the ark of the covenant?

• The rings on the ark were to hold the poles by which the priests would transport the ark of the covenant. When were the poles to be in the rings?

• What do you learn about the mercy seat?

• What do you learn from marking the pronouns that belong to God?

• Was the ark to be empty?

14 "You shall put the poles into the rings on the sides of the ark, to carry the ark with them.

15 "The poles shall remain in the rings of the ark; they shall not be removed from it....

17 "You shall make a mercy seat of pure gold, two and a half cubits long and one and a half cubits wide.

18 "You shall make two cherubim of gold, make them of hammered work at the two ends of the mercy seat.

19 "Make one cherub at one end and one cherub at the other end; you shall make the cherubim of one piece with the mercy seat at its two ends.

20 "The cherubim shall have their wings spread upward, covering the mercy seat with their wings and facing one another; the faces of the cherubim are to be turned toward the mercy seat.

21 "You shall put the mercy seat on top of the ark, and in the ark you shall put the testimony which I will give to you.

22 "There I will meet with you; and from above the mercy seat, from between the two cherubim which are upon the ark of the testimony, I will speak to you about all that I will give you in commandment for the sons of Israel."

OBSERVE

Our next passage will tell us what was to be put into the ark of the covenant.

Leader: Read Hebrews 9:3-4, reprinted on page 61.
- *Mark every reference to the **ark**.*
- *Also mark every reference to the **veil**.*

INSIGHT

In the Greek, *altar* in Hebrews 9:4 is literally "censer." The golden censer was taken into the Holy of Holies on the day of atonement. If incense was not taken off the altar of incense in the holy place and taken into the Holy of Holies, the priest would die. Exodus 31:11 and Leviticus 16:12-13 make it clear that the altar of incense was in the holy place in front of the veil.

DISCUSS

In Exodus you read that certain things were eventually placed into the ark of the covenant.

- Where was the ark of the covenant placed?

- According to this passage in Hebrews, what was placed in the ark of the covenant? Have the group number these three things in the text with a 1, 2, 3.

OBSERVE

The high priest entered the Holy of Holies only one time a year on Yom Kippur, the Day of Atonement. This happened on the tenth day of the seventh month of the Jewish calendar. Although this high and holy day is celebrated by Jewish people around the world, it is not celebrated in the way prescribed in Leviticus 16 simply because they have no temple—yet!

HEBREWS 9:3-4

3 Behind the second veil there was a tabernacle which is called the Holy of Holies,

4 having a golden altar of incense and the ark of the covenant covered on all sides with gold, in which was a golden jar holding the manna, and Aaron's rod which budded, and the tables of the covenant.

LEVITICUS 16:11-17,34

11 "Then Aaron shall offer the bull of the sin offering which is for himself and make atonement for himself and for his household, and he shall slaughter the bull of the sin offering which is for himself.

12 "He shall take a firepan full of coals of fire from upon the altar before the LORD and two handfuls of finely ground sweet incense, and bring it inside the veil.

13 "He shall put the incense on the fire before the LORD, that the cloud of incense may cover the mercy seat that is on the ark of the testimony, otherwise he will die.

Leader: Read to the group Leviticus 16:11-17,34.

- *Underline* **mercy seat** *as you have before.*
- *Mark every reference to* **Aaron** *with a* **P.**
- *Mark* **blood** *like this:* blood

Leader: Now read through this passage again and mark the following:

- *Mark every reference to* **sin** *with a big* **S.**
- *Mark* **atonement** *with a half circle.*
- *Put a clock over every reference to* **time.**

DISCUSS

- What does Aaron do for himself in verses 11-14? Discuss the procedure or have someone act out (at the group's instructions) what the priest did on the Day of Atonement in respect to the mercy seat.

- What does Aaron as the high priest do for the people, as recorded in verses 15-17?

- What do you learn from marking *atonement*? Make sure you see why atonement is necessary and for whom atonement is made and how.

- Did this ceremony cover, make atonement, for the sins of the people for all time? How do you know from the text?

- Was anyone with the high priest in the Holy of Holies, or even in the tent of meeting, when he did this on the day of atonement?

14 "Moreover, he shall take some of the blood of the bull and sprinkle it with his finger on the mercy seat on the east side; also in front of the mercy seat he shall sprinkle some of the blood with his finger seven times.

15 "Then he shall slaughter the goat of the sin offering which is for the people, and bring its blood inside the veil and do with its blood as he did with the blood of the bull, and sprinkle it on the mercy seat and in front of the mercy seat.

16 "He shall make atonement for the holy place, because of the impurities of the sons of Israel and because of their transgressions in

regard to all their sins; and thus he shall do for the tent of meeting which abides with them in the midst of their impurities.

17 "When he goes in to make atonement in the holy place, no one shall be in the tent of meeting until he comes out, that he may make atonement for himself and for his household and for all the assembly of Israel.…

34 "Now you shall have this as a permanent statute, to make atonement for the sons of Israel for all their sins once every year." And just as the LORD had commanded Moses, so he did.

OBSERVE

As our great High Priest, what did Jesus do?

Leader: Read aloud Hebrews 9:11-12,24-25.
- *Mark every reference to **Christ** (Messiah) with a cross.*
- *Mark **blood.***
- *Put a clock over every reference to **time.***

DISCUSS

- What do you learn from marking the references to Jesus Christ?

- Where did Jesus enter? How did He enter?

• What did He obtain through the sacrifice of Himself?

• When you read all this, doesn't it make you want to bow low before Him? to worship Him, adore Him, give Him your all?

OBSERVE

Leader: Read aloud Hebrews 2:17 and 1 John 2:1-2.

- *Mark every reference to **Jesus Christ, our High Priest**, with a cross.*
- *Mark **propitiation** as you marked "atonement."*
- *Mark **sin.***

HEBREWS 9:11-12,24-25

11 But when Christ appeared as a high priest of the good things to come, He entered through the greater and more perfect tabernacle, not made with hands, that is to say, not of this creation;

12 and not through the blood of goats and calves, but through His own blood, He entered the holy place once for all, having obtained eternal redemption....

24 For Christ did not enter a holy place made with hands, a mere copy of the true one, but into heaven itself, now to appear in the presence of God for us;

25 nor was it that He would offer Himself often, as the high priest enters the holy place year by year with blood that is not his own.

HEBREWS 2:17

Therefore, He had to be made like His brethren in all things, so that He might become a merciful and faithful high priest in things pertaining to God, to make propitiation for the sins of the people.

1 JOHN 2:1-2

1 My little children, I am writing these things to you so that you may not sin. And if anyone sins, we have an Advocate with the Father, Jesus Christ the righteous;

INSIGHT

The Greek word translated *propitiation* in 1 John 2:2 is *hilasmos.* It signifies a means whereby sin is covered and remitted. Because Jesus was able to pay for all our sins in full, God's holiness is satisfied. Jesus is our "mercy seat"—the propitiation for our sins—the full payment, which is sufficient for all time.

DISCUSS

• What did Jesus do in regard to our sins?

• What does Jesus become to us before the Father?

• Whose sins did Jesus propitiate (pay for), according to these verses?

• Is that good news? Does it make you want to worship Him—to fall before Him in thanksgiving that you have this good news to bring to a lost world? There *is* forgiveness for those who will believe.

OBSERVE

Isn't this awesome? But wait, there's more!

Leader: Read aloud Matthew 27:51 and Hebrews 10:19-23.
- *Mark every reference to **Jesus**.*
- *Mark every reference to the **veil**.*
- *Circle every reference to the **brethren**.*

The verses in Matthew are an account of Jesus' crucifixion, and the verses in Hebrews explain the significance of what happened to the veil when Jesus died.

INSIGHT

Josephus, a Jewish historian, wrote that the veil in the temple was so thick that it would take two teams of oxen pulling in opposite directions to tear it. It is interesting to note that we are told the veil was torn from top to bottom, not vice versa.

2 and He Himself is the propitiation for our sins; and not for ours only, but also for those of the whole world.

MATTHEW 27:51

And behold, the veil of the temple was torn in two from top to bottom; and the earth shook and the rocks were split.

HEBREWS 10:19-23

19 Therefore, brethren, since we have confidence to enter the holy place by the blood of Jesus,

20 by a new and living way which He inaugurated for us through the veil, that is, His flesh,

21 and since we have a great priest over the house of God,

22 let us draw near with a sincere heart in full assurance of faith, having our hearts sprinkled clean from an evil conscience and our bodies washed with pure water.

23 Let us hold fast the confession of our hope without wavering, for He who promised is faithful.

DISCUSS

At the beginning of this week's lesson, we saw from Hebrews 10:20 that the veil was a picture of Jesus' flesh.

• If the ark of the covenant represented the throne of God and the veil in the tabernacle and in the temple kept the priest from entering into the Holy of Holies except on the day of atonement, what is God picturing for us when He tears the veil in two from top to bottom?

• In John 14:6, Jesus says that He is the way, the truth, and the life and that no one comes to the Father but through Him. How is this supported in the picture of the veil torn in two?

• What does all this mean to us—the brethren?

• Where are you, as a child of God, allowed to go that not even the high priest could go except on the Day of Atonement? Why are you allowed so great a privilege? What does it make you want to do?

• How does Hebrews 10:21-22 relate to what you have learned about the tabernacle and worship?

WRAP IT UP

Because of the finished work of the Lord Jesus Christ, you are cleansed once and for all and are now able to enter into the very throne room of God and find grace to help in the time of need.

What more could one ask for? There is no greater privilege than to have unhindered access to the throne of the Most High God through His only begotten Son, who loves you so much that He laid down His life for you when you were a sinner, without hope, ungodly—an enemy of God.

What can you do but bow before Him in worship, presenting yourself as a living sacrifice—holy, acceptable to God—which is but your reasonable worship of service!

Wrap up these truths in prayer, beloved of God, by worshiping the Lord, thanking Him and praising Him for all you have learned and what it means to you personally.

And while the others pray, if you have not yet received Jesus Christ as your Lord—is now the time to repent, to have a change of mind, and do so? To believe on the Lord Jesus Christ who won so great a salvation for you? To be born again—born from above—born into the forever family of God? If so, simply tell God that you believe and that you want to become His child. His arms are open wide—as wide as on a cross.

Therefore, since we have a great high priest who
has passed through the heavens,
Jesus the Son of God, let us hold fast our confession.

For we do not have a high priest who cannot
sympathize with our weaknesses,
but One who has been tempted in all things
as we are, yet without sin.
Therefore let us draw near with confidence to the throne of grace,
so that we may receive mercy and find grace to help in time of need.

HEBREWS 4:14-16

The people of Israel worshiped God as they kept the feasts and brought their sacrifices to the temple in Jerusalem—but that was before Jesus became the mediator of a New Covenant. How—and where—are those who are now members of the body of Christ to worship God? What is our worship of God to look like? What form is it to take?

This is what we will look at in our final week of study.

OBSERVE

Our first study passage this week includes a reference to a Samaritan woman. The Samaritans were descended from Jews who intermarried with their Assyrian captors after the northern kingdom was conquered in 722 B.C. These particular Jews were left behind by the Assyrians because they were not considered valuable enough to take home as the spoils of war.

In Jesus' day, the Jews hated the Samaritans, who were considered half-breeds. Part Jew and part Gentile, the Samaritans couldn't prove their Israelite genealogy. The Jews avoided them at all cost and therefore wouldn't travel through Samaria, which lay between Jerusalem and Galilee.

Thus the Samaritans, after being rejected by the Jews, established their own temple and religious services on Mount Gerizim.

Jesus and His disciples could have taken two other routes to Galilee from Jerusalem, but Jesus chose to pass directly through Samaria. After the disciples went into town to find something to eat, Jesus waited at Jacob's well for their return. As He was sitting at the well, a woman of

JOHN 4:9-29

⁹ Therefore the Samaritan woman said to Him, "How is it that You, being a Jew, ask me for a drink since I am a Samaritan woman?" (For Jews have no dealings with Samaritans.)

¹⁰ Jesus answered and said to her, "If you knew the gift of God, and who it is who says to you, 'Give Me a drink,' you would have asked Him, and He would have given you living water."

¹¹ She said to Him, "Sir, You have nothing to draw with and the well is deep; where then do You get that living water?

Samaria came to draw water. Jesus knew more about her than she could ever have imagined.

As she approached the well, Jesus asked her for a drink.

Leader: Read aloud John 4:9-29. As you read, have the group pay careful attention to what is transpiring in these verses—the charged atmosphere right from the beginning of their encounter.

- *Mark every reference to the **water** Jesus gives:* ‿‿‿‿‿‿
- *Mark every reference to **worship** with a* **W.**

INSIGHT

The word *worship* in this passage is the Greek word *proskuneo*. It means to kiss the hand, to fall on the knees, or to be prostrate on the ground. It also could mean to express respect or to show obedience, honor, or reverence to a divine being.

DISCUSS

Leader: *These questions are simply to help you get a discussion started that will help the group see what it means to worship God in spirit and in truth. Use them as they suit your group.*

• What do you learn from marking *worship*? (Move through the verses one by one.)

• When Jesus mentioned water that would quench her thirst, what was the Samaritan woman focused on? What kind of water?

• What was Jesus talking about when He mentioned living water? The literal or the spiritual?

12 "You are not greater than our father Jacob, are You, who gave us the well, and drank of it himself and his sons and his cattle?"

13 Jesus answered and said to her, "Everyone who drinks of this water will thirst again;

14 but whoever drinks of the water that I will give him shall never thirst; but the water that I will give him will become in him a well of water springing up to eternal life."

15 The woman said to Him, "Sir, give me this water, so I will not be thirsty nor come all the way here to draw."

16 He said to her, "Go, call your husband and come here."

17 The woman answered and said, "I have no husband." Jesus said to her, "You have correctly said, 'I have no husband';

18 for you have had five husbands, and the one whom you now have is not your husband; this you have said truly."

19 The woman said to Him, "Sir, I perceive that You are a prophet.

20 "Our fathers worshiped in this mountain, and you people say that in Jerusalem is the place where men ought to worship."

21 Jesus said to her, "Woman, believe Me, an hour is coming when neither in this

• When the woman and Jesus talked about worship, was the Samaritan woman thinking of spiritual or physical worship? How do you know?

• What time do you think Jesus was referring to when He said that the hour was coming when the Father would not be worshiped at Gerizim or in Jerusalem? Jesus knew the veil would be torn in two—that there would be a new and living way to enter into the holy place and worship God. He also knew (and would foretell) of the destruction of Jerusalem and the temple. This occurred in A.D. 70, and there hasn't been a temple since then. So where and how would they worship?

• In the context of this account, what do you think it means to worship God in spirit? Was the Samaritan woman worshiping God in spirit? Where was her focus?

• If the Samaritans were not going to Jerusalem to worship in the temple in the way God prescribed under the Old Covenant, were they worshiping Him in truth? (For example, God had given specific instructions that the temple was to be built in Jerusalem. The Samaritans chose Mount Gerizim because they recognized only the Torah, the first five books of the Bible, as being the Word of God while the Jews accepted the entire Hebrew canon, what we call the Old Testament.)

mountain nor in Jerusalem will you worship the Father.

22 "You worship what you do not know; we worship what we know, for salvation is from the Jews.

23 "But an hour is coming, and now is, when the true worshipers will worship the Father in spirit and truth; for such people the Father seeks to be His worshipers.

24 "God is spirit, and those who worship Him must worship in spirit and truth."

25 The woman said to Him, "I know that Messiah is coming (He who is called Christ); when that One comes,

He will declare all things to us."

26 Jesus said to her, "I who speak to you am He."

27 At this point His disciples came, and they were amazed that He had been speaking with a woman, yet no one said, "What do You seek?" or, "Why do You speak with her?"

28 So the woman left her waterpot, and went into the city and said to the men,

29 "Come, see a man who told me all the things that I have done; this is not the Christ, is it?"

• Under the New Covenant, has God given us, as believers in Jesus Christ, a prescribed method of worship? a prescribed place? According to these verses in John 4, how are we to worship God properly?

• According to John 4:24, what is God?

• What do you think it means to worship God in truth? Where does someone find truth?

OBSERVE

True worship is not a matter of externals, of rituals, but of the spirit—it's not a matter of the body or of the soul—although both might participate in worship; rather true worship engages the spirit of man.

In Philippians 3:2-3, Paul contrasts the false circumcision, that of the flesh—the external rite—with the true circumcision of the heart as promised in the New Covenant in Jeremiah 31.

Leader: *Read aloud Philippians 3:2-3.*
  • *Mark the word **worship**.*

DISCUSS

• What is contrasted in verses 2 and 3?

• In verse 3, you see the contrast between worshiping in the Spirit of God and glorying in Christ Jesus and in putting your confidence where?

• When you personally worship God, what do you put your confidence in? Is it in the flesh—the feeling and the experiences of the flesh, the posture of the flesh—or in your heart, in the inner man that wants to honor God as God, to respect Him, to obey Him—to commune with Him?

PHILIPPIANS 3:2-3

2 Beware of the dogs, beware of the evil workers, beware of the false circumcision;

3 for we are the true circumcision, who worship in the Spirit of God and glory in Christ Jesus and put no confidence in the flesh.

JOHN 17:15-19

15 "I do not ask You to take them out of the world, but to keep them from the evil one.

16 "They are not of the world, even as I am not of the world.

17 "Sanctify them in the truth; Your word is truth.

18 "As You sent Me into the world, I also have sent them into the world.

19 "For their sakes I sanctify Myself, that they themselves also may be sanctified in truth.

OBSERVE

How vital is truth in the life of a child of God? Being truthful with ourselves— speaking the truth in love to one another— walking in the truth—earnestly contending for the faith, the truth? Worshiping God in truth?

Leader: Read John 17:15-19, a portion of the prayer Jesus prayed as He left the upper room and made His way to Gethsemane. His hour had finally come as the Lamb of God who would take away the sins of the world. Now His concern is those who believe on His name.

• *Mark the words* **sanctify** *and* **sanctified** *with a cloud.*

• *Underline every occurrence of* **truth.**

DISCUSS

• What do you learn from marking the references to *truth*?

• How are we sanctified (made holy, set apart, consecrated to God)?

• In light of what you have observed, how important is truth?

• How critical is truth if you are going to worship God properly? Can you give some examples or illustrations?

OBSERVE

Leader: Read Mark 7:6-9, 13.

• *Circle every reference to the **people** including the personal pronouns **they, their, you,** and **your.***
• *Mark the word **worship.***
• *Mark the word **tradition** with a* **T.**
• *Mark every reference to the **commandment of God** and the **word of God** like this:* ▱▱

DISCUSS

Leader: Once again, choose those questions that will precipitate a discussion, cover the text, and help the group see the importance of worshiping God in truth.

MARK 7:6-9,13

6 And He said to them, "Rightly did Isaiah prophesy of you hypocrites, as it is written: 'This people honors Me with their lips, But their heart is far away from Me.

7 'But in vain do they worship Me, Teaching as doctrines the precepts of men.'

8 "Neglecting the commandment of God, you hold to the tradition of men."

9 He was also saying to them, "You are experts at setting aside the commandment of God in order to keep your tradition.

13 thus invalidating the word of God by your tradition which you have handed down; and you do many things such as that."

• What do you learn from marking the references to the people?

• What do you learn from marking *tradition* and the *word* and *commandment of God*?

• What do you learn about their worship of God?

• How did the people invalidate the Word of God?

• Can you see any way in which this is occurring today?

• What do you see people gravitating to today? Are they focused on the emotional, the sensational, the experiential, the testimonies and latest faddish teachings, or on the clear and systematic teaching of the Word of God? Why do you think this is so? How would either of these trends affect their worship?

• Have you ever evaluated the way you worship God—the worship songs you sing, the way you approach God in prayer, the things you claim in prayer, the way you dress, the way you treat people, the way you behave, the standards you hold—against the character of God and the whole counsel of His Word? How critical is this to being a true worshiper of God?

• If we are going to worship God in truth, how willing do you think we ought to be to stand for the integrity of the Word of God in our corporate worship?

WRAP IT UP

The enemy of our soul will do everything he can to keep us from worshiping God in spirit and truth. He offered Jesus all the kingdoms of this world if He would only bow down and worship him (Matthew 4:8-10).

How we need to be aware of the subtleties of prosperity and ease, which can cause us to forget the greatness of our God and the so-great-a-salvation He has wrought for us! And when we do forget, our worship will become mechanical just as Israel's did. Even though they were explicitly warned by Moses in Deuteronomy 6:10-15, they worshiped God only with their lips while their hearts were far from Him.

When Jesus was tempted by the devil, He once again reminded Satan of the truth recorded in this passage from Deuteronomy when He said: "It is written, 'You shall worship the LORD your God and serve Him only'" (Matthew 4:10).

True worshipers worship the Father in spirit and truth. Remember the Father is seeking people like this. May you be among them. Worship Him…in spirit and in truth…and in the beauty of holiness. Let your speech, your behavior, your character, your dress, your demeanor all testify that you are a true worshiper of the one and only true God.

Worship the LORD in holy attire;
Tremble before Him, all the earth.
Say among the nations, "The LORD reigns;
Indeed, the world is firmly established, it will not be moved;

He will judge the peoples with equity."
Let the heavens be glad, and let the earth rejoice;
Let the sea roar, and all it contains;
Let the field exult, and all that is in it.
Then all the trees of the forest will sing for joy
Before the LORD, for He is coming,
For He is coming to judge the earth.
He will judge the world in righteousness
And the peoples in His faithfulness.

PSALM 96:9-13

40 MINUTE BIBLE STUDIES

No-Homework
That Help You

A 6-WEEK, NO-HOMEWORK BIBLE STUDY
MORE THAN 700,000 SOLD IN THE SERIES

Being a Disciple:
Counting the Real Cost

Kay Arthur, Tom & Jane Hart

PRECEPT MINISTRIES INTERNATIONAL

A 6-WEEK, NO-HOMEWORK BIBLE STUDY
MORE THAN 700,000 SOLD IN THE SERIES

Building a
Marriage **That Really Works**

Kay Arthur, David & BJ Lawson

PRECEPT MINISTRIES INTERNATIONAL

A 6-WEEK, NO-HOMEWORK BIBLE STUDY
MORE THAN 700,000 SOLD IN THE SERIES

How to Make
Choices **You Won't Regret**

Kay Arthur, David & BJ Lawson

PRECEPT MINISTRIES INTERNATIONAL

A 6-WEEK, NO-HOMEWORK BIBLE STUDY
MORE THAN 700,000 SOLD IN THE SERIES

A Man's Strategy
For Conquering
Temptation

Bob Vereen

PRECEPT MINISTRIES INTERNATIONAL

A 6-WEEK, NO-HOMEWORK BIBLE STUDY
MORE THAN 700,000 SOLD IN THE SERIES

Living
Victoriously in
Difficult Times

Kay Arthur, Bob & Diane Vereen

PRECEPT MINISTRIES INTERNATIONAL

A 6-WEEK, NO-HOMEWORK BIBLE STUDY
MORE THAN 700,000 SOLD IN THE SERIES

Discovering
What the
Future Holds

Kay Arthur & Georg Huber

PRECEPT MINISTRIES INTERNATIONAL

A 6-WEEK, NO-HOMEWORK BIBLE STUDY
MORE THAN 700,000 SOLD IN THE SERIES

Key Principles
of Biblical
Fasting

Kay Arthur & Pete DeLacy

PRECEPT MINISTRIES INTERNATIONAL

A 6-WEEK, NO-HOMEWORK BIBLE STUDY
MORE THAN 700,000 SOLD IN THE SERIES

Forgiveness:
Breaking the Power of the Past

Kay Arthur, David & BJ Lawson

PRECEPT MINISTRIES INTERNATIONAL

Bible Studies
Discover Truth For Yourself

A 6-WEEK, NO-HOMEWORK BIBLE STUDY
MORE THAN 700,000 SOLD IN THE SERIES

How Do You Know God's Your Father?

Kay Arthur, David & BJ Lawson

PRECEPT MINISTRIES INTERNATIONAL
40minute BIBLE STUDY

A 6-WEEK, NO-HOMEWORK BIBLE STUDY
MORE THAN 700,000 SOLD IN THE SERIES

How Do You Walk the Walk You Talk?

Kay Arthur

PRECEPT MINISTRIES INTERNATIONAL
40minute BIBLE STUDY

A 6-WEEK, NO-HOMEWORK BIBLE STUDY
MORE THAN 700,000 SOLD IN THE SERIES

Money and Possessions: The Quest for Contentment

Kay Arthur & David Arthur

PRECEPT MINISTRIES INTERNATIONAL
40minute BIBLE STUDY

A 6-WEEK, NO-HOMEWORK BIBLE STUDY
MORE THAN 700,000 SOLD IN THE SERIES

The Essentials of Effective Prayer

Kay Arthur, David & BJ Lawson

PRECEPT MINISTRIES INTERNATIONAL
40minute BIBLE STUDY

A 6-WEEK, NO-HOMEWORK BIBLE STUDY
MORE THAN 700,000 SOLD IN THE SERIES

Having a Real Relationship with God

Kay Arthur

PRECEPT MINISTRIES INTERNATIONAL
40minute BIBLE STUDY

A 6-WEEK, NO-HOMEWORK BIBLE STUDY
MORE THAN 700,000 SOLD IN THE SERIES

Rising to the Call of Leadership

Kay Arthur, David & BJ Lawson

PRECEPT MINISTRIES INTERNATIONAL
40minute BIBLE STUDY

A 6-WEEK, NO-HOMEWORK BIBLE STUDY
MORE THAN 700,000 SOLD IN THE SERIES

What Does the Bible Say About Sex?

Kay Arthur, David & BJ Lawson

PRECEPT MINISTRIES INTERNATIONAL
40minute BIBLE STUDY

A 6-WEEK, NO-HOMEWORK BIBLE STUDY
MORE THAN 700,000 SOLD IN THE SERIES

Living a Life of True Worship

Kay Arthur, Bob & Diane Vereen

PRECEPT MINISTRIES INTERNATIONAL
40minute BIBLE STUDY

Another powerful study series from beloved Bible teacher

{ A Devotional Study on Living by Faith }

LORD, Where Are You When Bad Things Happen?

KAY ARTHUR

{ A Devotional Study on Growing in Character from The Beatitudes }

LORD, Only You Can Change Me

KAY ARTHUR

{ A Devotional Study on Spiritual Victory }

LORD, Is It Warfare? Teach Me to Stand

KAY ARTHUR

{ A Devotional Study on the Names of God }

LORD, I Want to Know You

KAY ARTHUR

{ A Devotional Study on God's Power for Daily Living }

LORD, I Need Grace to Make It Today

KAY ARTHUR

KAY ARTHUR

The Lord series provides insightful, warm-hearted Bible studies designed to meet you where you are —and help you discover God's answers to your deepest needs.

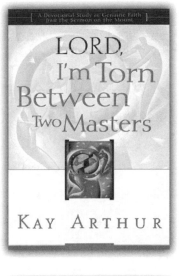

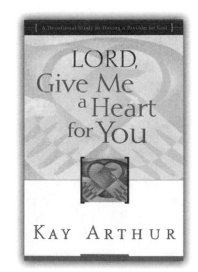

ALSO AVAILABLE:
One-year devotionals to draw you closer to the heart of God.

ABOUT KAY ARTHUR AND PRECEPT MINISTRIES INTERNATIONAL

KAY ARTHUR is known around the world as an international Bible teacher, author, conference speaker, and host of the national radio and television programs *Precepts for Life*, which reaches a worldwide viewing audience of over 94 million. A four-time Gold Medallion Award–winning author, Kay has authored more than 100 books and Bible studies.

Kay and her husband, Jack, founded Precept Ministries International in 1970 in Chattanooga, Tennessee, with a vision to establish people in God's Word. Today, the ministry has a worldwide outreach. In addition to inductive study training workshops and thousands of small-group studies across America, PMI reaches nearly 150 countries with inductive Bible studies translated into nearly 70 languages, teaching people to discover Truth for themselves.

Contact Precept Ministries International for more information about inductive Bible studies in your area.

Precept Ministries International
P.O. Box 182218
Chattanooga, TN 37422-7218
800-763-8280
www.precept.org

ABOUT BOB AND DIANE VEREEN

BOB AND DIANE VEREEN serve as ambassadors-at-large for Precept Ministries International, speaking at conferences around the world and overseeing a number of Precept's international offices. They both travel the globe teaching people how to study the Bible inductively as well as mentoring and training national leadership. They have been on staff since 1991, following sixteen years of prior involvement with Precept Ministries International. Bob was a contributor to *The New Inductive Study Bible* and has written for the New Inductive Study Series and the 40-Minute Bible Studies series.